A Touch of Grace
The G.R.A.C.E. Ministries Story

By

Ruth Fowler
with B. J. Bassett

Copyright © 2010 by Ruth Fowler with B. J. Bassett

A Touch of Grace
The G.R.A.C.E. Ministries Story
by Ruth Fowler with B. J. Bassett

Printed in the United States of America

ISBN 9781612155746

All rights reserved solely by the author. The author guarantees all contents are original and do not infringe upon the legal rights of any other person or work. No part of this book may be reproduced in any form without the permission of the author. The views expressed in this book are not necessarily those of the publisher.

Unless otherwise indicated, Bible quotations are taken from The King James Bible; The American Standard Version of the Bible; The Revised Standard Version of the Bible. Copyright © Old Testament 1952; New Testament 1946, 1971 by Zondervan Publishing House, Inc.; The New American Standard Version of the Bible. Updated Edition. Copyright © 1999 by The Zondervan Corporation; The New International Version of the Bible. Copyright © 1990 by The Zondervan Corporation; and The New King James Version of the Bible. Copyright © 1979, 1980, 1982 by Thomas Nelson, Inc.

www.xulonpress.com

Day by day

Dear Lord of Thee three things I pray

To see you more clearly

To love you more dearly

To follow you more nearly

Richard of Chichester
(1197-1253)

Table of Contests

Part I

The History of G.R.A.C.E. Ministries

Introduction 13
The Desires of My Heart 15
Stay Vanilla 28
One Day You Will Lead This Ministry 41
G.R.A.C.E. G.U.Y.S. 52

Part II

He Touched Me— Stories of Women Changed by God through G.R.A.C.E. Ministries

In Memory of LaDonna 59
Lois's Story 60
Sherry's Story 61

Pat's Story 64

Diane's Story 66

Madge's Story 68

Robin's Story 69

Vicki's Story 72

Ulla's Story 76

Jane's Story 79

Shirley J's Story 81

Judy's Story 88

Shirley K's Story 93

Jackie's Story 95

Part III

What Makes Me a Christian? 107

How to Become a Christian 109

How to Write Your Story 112

Afterward 115

Dedication

In loving memory of my brother Ed and his lovely wife Nancy, who made G.R.A.C.E. Ministries possible. To God be the glory both now and forever more.

R.F.

To my darling daughters, Dawn, Kathy, Melanie, and daughter-in-law, Ana – women I admire, love and respect.

B.J.B.

Part I

Introduction

When Ruth asked me to help her write a book on the history of G.R.A.C.E. (Greater Roseburg Area Committee for Evangelism) Ministries, I told her I'd have to think about it and get back to her. At the time I was writing a nonfiction book I wasn't passionate about—so it wasn't a difficult decision to put that project on the back burner. Yet, I also had three novels, in varying stages, which I was passionate about. I saw in Ruth how important the book on G.R.A.C.E. Ministries was to her, so I agreed to help her.

The story of G.R.A.C.E. Ministries began when Ruth celebrated her fiftieth birthday. She prayed, *"Lord, I want the last part of my life to count for the Kingdom."* Part of her prayer, *Let My Life Count for the Kingdom*, became the working title of the book and is a thread that runs through it.

All of the stories recorded in *A Touch of Grace* are written by humble ordinary women with a desire to serve their extraordinary God. Part I is the history of G.R.A.C.E. Ministries, Part II contains testimonies of how God changed lives through the ministry. Part III consists of "How to Become a Christian" and "How to Write Your Story."

I've been blessed by these women, their faith and their stories, and I think you'll be blessed too. You'll meet women who have suffered from abuse, divorce, depression, and the loss of a child.

Most of them didn't feel qualified or worthy to serve in leadership, yet they all surrendered to God's will and put their complete trust in Him. They let go and let God and were touched by His grace.

B. J. Bassett

The Desires of My Heart
Ruth's Story

"Delight thyself also in the Lord; and he shall give thee the desires of thine heart." Psalm 37:4 KJV.

My story begins before I was born. My parents were Christians and their only daughter began to pray for the desire of her heart – a brother and a baby sister. Her prayer was answered when my brother was born and eventually I joined the family in 1927, I'm the baby sister.

My dad was wealthy as a building contractor, owning a lot of property in the bay area in northern California. My mother wanted to tithe, but Dad was firm. "It's too much money," he said.

We moved to Alturas, California, and my dad continued to build. It was the middle of the great depression and my parents experienced a difficult time when one of my dad's employees sued him. Dad didn't hire an attorney to represent him and he suffered a great loss. It was during this time that my mother had a dream. In her dream, water covered everything except a house on a hill. God spoke to her in her dream, *"Do you want houses and lands, or my love?"* My mother chose God's love. It was soon after her dream that my parents began to tithe.

In that dream, God gave my mother a choice and I've always been grateful she chose God's love over houses and land. I was blessed to be raised by a very wise Christian Mother. It was at her knee that I asked Jesus into my heart when I was five. Jesus was always special to me and, with a child's understanding, I always felt drawn to Him. At fourteen I had another encounter thru the Holy Spirit and He became Lord of my life.

Later came the busy years of life— marriage, home, children— and as much as I loved Jesus I did not develop daily habits of devotion. It took the tragic death of my baby daughter for me to begin my daily devotional life. Not until we moved to Roseburg in 1965 and I became involved with Bible Study Fellowship did my daily walk in the word become purposeful. *"But seek ye first the kingdom of God, and His righteousness; and all these things shall be added unto you." Matthew 6:33 KJV.* These were no longer words to me. They were the very Words of God.

My husband, Dick, and I were content with life as it was. Yet in 1974, in a rather miraculous way, we purchased Bible Book Center in Roseburg, Oregon. So began an eighteen year pilgrimage for us. Only God could have brought about the change in our lives.

I'm sure my parents' Christian example during my childhood, including tithing, influenced my life. Yet it was many years later that I felt convicted to tithe myself. Dick and I struggled with financial concerns. I felt God nudge me to begin by tithing my grocery money. Later Dick joined me in tithing as well. It was W.T. "Bill" Carlson's book, *The Sharecropper*, which ministered to me about what it means to give. I'm a firm believer that our tithe always belongs to our individual churches. Anything over and above our tithe is an offering which can be donated to ministries we feel passionate about.

With my children raised, I celebrated my 50th birthday and prayed, *"Lord, I want the last part of my life to count for the Kingdom."*

Like other faithful followers of Jesus Christ, my walk with the Lord changed and grew over the years. I felt He wanted me to be His Emissary. (An Emissary is a person sent on a mission, a secret agent, employed to ascertain the opinions of others, and to spread reports or propagate opinions favorable to his employer or designed to defeat the measures or schemes of his opposers or foes; a spy; but an emissary may differ from a spy, an emissary may be a secret agent employed not only to detect the schemes of the opposing party, but to influence their councils; and an emissary may in some cases be known as the agent of an adversary, without incurring hazard, exploring or spying.)

I was about to be sent on a mission, and the territory God wanted me to serve Him in was unfamiliar to me and at that time, I didn't feel qualified. While I had taught children in Sunday school, I didn't consider myself capable to teach adults. But God was nudging me in that direction. My husband, Dick, supported my decisions to get away and pray. He parked our trailer along the Oregon Coast and left me there for a week to spend time with God in prayer. It was during that time that I looked out to sea and got the answer I was searching for. Ella Wheeler Wilcox's poem, *Winds of Fate*, ministered to me at that time of decision.

Winds of Fate
One ship drives east
And another drives west,
With the self- same winds that blow;
'Tis the set of the sails, and not the gales,
Which tell us the way to go.

Like the winds of the sea are the ways of fate.
As we voyage along through life;
'Tis the set of the soul that decides the goal,
And not the calm or the strife.

Like other testimonies recorded in this book, I needed to let go and let God do what I didn't think I could possibly do. It was then that I spent five years in Bible Study Fellowship where I continued to grow.

Over the years I'd attended many women's conferences and, as a Christian bookstore owner, Christian Booksellers Conventions. I sat in packed auditoriums listening to well known Christian speakers like Corrie ten Boom and Phillip Keller, author of *A Shepherd Looks at Psalm 23*. I was fortunate to be able to travel to Denver, Colorado twice and experience spiritual highs. I'd come home and want to share with other women the blessings I'd received, but second hand sharing isn't the same as experiencing it first hand. So I began to pray for the women living in Douglas County. I prayed for fourteen years.

I wrote to Evelyn Christenson, the author of *What Happens When Women Pray,* and asked her to come and speak to the women in Roseburg. She graciously said she'd file my request. I bought all her tapes and books and began a women's Bible study at my church. It changed women's lives, but what more can I do? I kept praying.

*　*　*

Both my sister, Irene, and my brother had traveled to Finland, the homeland of our heritage. Then it was my turn to go. My brother, who was always generous to me, sent a check for an all expense paid trip to Finland. I returned home with money left over from that memorable trip.

In 1987 I took a carload of women from the Roseburg area to an OASIS women's conference in Salem, Oregon. My burden for the women in Roseburg never wavered. I felt they needed to hear Lin Ludwick, one of the conference workshop leaders who spoke at that conference.

That day, during lunch, the ladies I'd brought from Roseburg discussed how inspirational Lin Ludwick's workshop was. We agreed that we needed to get her to come to Roseburg and speak. We prayed together.

After we returned home, we continued to pray, meet, plan and fast. The board was made up of housewives mostly. At the meeting we discussed how we'd get the word out, someone said, "I can do that." Or, when asked who would be responsible for the details of the luncheon, another volunteered, "I can do that." Others took care of mailings and telephoning. Several offered to bake pies as a fund raiser. I donated the seed money (from what was left from my Finland trip.) I gave the money and God blessed it. Everyone at that meeting jumped in and took on a different responsibility in the organization of G.R.A.C.E. (Greater Roseburg Area Committee for Evangelism) Ministries.

"Now there are diversities of gifts, but the same Spirit. And there are differences of administrations, but the same Lord serving. There are many ways in which God works in our lives, but it is the same God who does the work in and through all of us who are his." 1 Corinthians 12: 4-6 KJV. God used each of us with our own giftedness, yet G.R.A.C.E. Ministries was never one persons. It was the Lords.

The committee members represented five different churches, so we decided to hold an annual conference at different churches each year, making it an interdenominational ministry. That was our original intent and it has remained interdenominational over the years.

In 1987 Roseburg was suffering difficult times with the lumber business declining, people out of work, businesses closing and the gas crunch. Women couldn't afford to go to a conference. A decision was made in the beginning and continues to this day. G.R.A.C.E Ministries will not charge women to attend. Any monies received would come from donations and free will offerings, with some women, who are able, to put in extra.

The leadership committee prayed for six months before our first conference. We stressed prayer. It was then and is now the foundation of G.R.A.C.E. Ministries. We prayed for the local pastors and churches.

We also met with the pastors, assuring them that our goal was not to take the women away from their churches, but to bless them and encourage them to grow closer to God and serve Him in their church. .

Not having any idea how many would attend the conference, God assured me while praying, *"Despise not small beginnings."* Our first conference was held on March 1988 with about forty to fifty women. Lin Ludwick, the former Dean of Women at Multnomah School of the Bible, was the speaker.

With my connections as a Christian bookstore owner, speakers seemed to fall in my lap. I met speakers at the Christian Booksellers Convention, or I'd hear a speaker at a conference, or a publisher's representative would recommend someone.

* * *

The two books that ministered to me and became instrumental in the foundation of G.R.A.C.E. Ministries were *What Happens When Women Pray* by Evelyn Christenson and the other is *The Sharecropper* by W.T. "Bill" Carlson. Prayer and tithing were the catalyst for G.R.A.C.E. Ministries from the beginning.

"Bring ye all the tithes into the storehouse, that there may be meat in mine house, and prove me now herewith, saith the Lord of hosts, if I will not open you the windows of heaven, and pour you out a blessing, that there shall not be room enough to receive it." Malachi 3:10 KJV.

I take Malachi 3:10 literally— God truly opened the windows of heaven and poured out a blessing for G.R.A.C.E. Ministries from the beginning and continued to bless it over the years as well.

G.R.A.C.E. Ministries tithes offerings taken at the conferences to the needs in the Roseburg community; once they repaired a church bus, another time Hope Pregnancy Center received their tithe.

At one point an example of our financial accountability was sharing the cost for a speaker with the Seventh Day

Adventist. While our conferences were held on Friday evenings and Saturdays, the Seventh Day Adventists held a conference on Sundays using the same speaker. Thus sharing travel and lodging expenses for the speaker.

After ten years of serving in G.R.A.C.E. Ministries, it was time for me to pass the gavel. My husband suffered some health problems and I felt I needed to be more accessible to him. It was time to pass the gavel.

Thou hast done well to kneel and say,
"Since he who gave can take away,
And bid me suffer, I obey!"

Adelaide Anne Procter

Sue Haberly, one of the women I'd mentored over the years, took up the gavel and become the leader of G.R.A.C.E. Ministries. While mentoring Sue, I watched her grow from a shy, behind the scenes volunteer into the leader she is today. (You can read her story in chapter two.) I enjoyed being used by God as a mentor to women. He always gave me Scripture to share with them for whatever they are dealing with in their lives at the time.

I continue to pray, give financially and keep up-to-date on what is happening in G.R.A.C.E. Ministries. I'm always thrilled to hear about lives changed and souls saved for the kingdom. Way back in the beginning only God knew how G.R.A.C.E. Ministries would grow and change. Today G.R.A.C.E. G.U.Y.S. (chapter 4) is a vital offshoot as well as workshops in the spring each year which provide an outreach to women's needs. The workshops cover subjects such as divorce, addiction, depression, etc. Another branch of G.R.A.C.E. Ministries today is their mentoring women. They listen, pray and share biblical principles and practical helps.

* * *

Although raised in a Christian home my brother, Ed, didn't come to the Lord until later in life. Over the years my mother, sister and I prayed for him. Our hearts were heavy for his salvation. Before Ed passed away, I felt the Lord directing me to prepare a booklet for him. God even led me to the pictures to include. On the cover was a portrait of my mother, father and sister, Irene.

On the first page of the book I pasted a photo of Ed and me as children. He is holding my hand. *"Ed liked to tease*

Little Sister, Ruthie. But after he grew up he showed his love and care by his generosity to big sister, Irene, and little sister Ruthie."

The last page of the booklet was the most important. It consisted of a recent photo of Ed, Irene and me with the message, *"Now they have all grown old together. Big Sister Irene and Little Sister Ruthie want to make sure they will all spend eternity together. Mama, Papa, Baby Carolyn and Little Bud have all gone before, waiting to welcome the family."* (Baby Carolyn was the baby I lost and Little Bud was Ed's grandson.)

I included the familiar verses I had memorized from God's Word. *"That if thou shalt confess with thy mouth the Lord Jesus, and shalt believe in thine heart that God hath raised him from the dead, thou shalt be saved. For with the heart man believeth unto righteousness; and with the mouth confession is made unto salvation. For whosoever shall call upon the name of the Lord shall be saved." Romans 10:9-10, 13 KJV.*

I had obeyed God's nudge, mailed the book and waited.

Only days before Ed passed away I heard his voice, *"Tell Ruthie I'll meet her in heaven."*

After his passing I poured my heart out to God, *"Ed didn't do anything for you, Lord,"* I prayed. I heard God's voice, *"What about G.R.A.C.E. Ministries?"* That's when I realized it was Ed's generous gift to me that provided the initial funds for G.R.A.C.E. Ministries.

God not only gave my sister, Irene, the desires of her heart, but he gave me the desires of my heart too. To God be the glory. *"Not to us, O Lord, not to us, but to thy name give glory, for the sake of thy steadfast love and thy faithfulness!" Psalms 115:1 RSV.*

Little Ruthie with big brother Ed

Stay Vanilla
Sue's Story

"Listen to advice and accept instruction, that you may gain wisdom for the future." Proverbs 19:20 RSV.

I grew up in a non-Christian home where love was not displayed which caused me to feel unloved and emotionally abandoned. I would say you could label me as the least likely to succeed. But God had other plans and He brought Ruth Fowler into my life later when I was a shy young wife and mother of two sons. I am sure Ruth noticed me at the church's altar Sunday after Sunday as I knelt often, burdened for my husband's salvation. Ruth saw something different in me; my desire for more of God was evident in my life so Ruth took me under her wing and began to mentor me.

At first we met weekly for prayer, later it was monthly. "The Lord will peel you like an onion," Ruth said. She always had a nugget of godly advice or a Scripture verse for me. And she helped me develop cause and effect of prayer – sowing and reaping.

When Ruth returned from the OASIS Christian women's conference in Salem, Oregon, she explained that she would like to start a prayer group of women and asked me to be the prayer chairman. Her vision was to start a Christian women's conference in Roseburg, and prayer was the first step. G.R.A.C.E. Ministries was the beginning of a whole new world and life for me.

After the leadership team met for a while, we decided we needed a name. Ruth was going to the Oregon Coast for a few days. She said, "While I'm there I'll walk on the beach and pray about a name." The committee prayed for her while she was away, knowing that God was going to share something with her. She came to the next prayer time and told us that she only received the word "GRACE". We loved it! Ideas whirled in our minds and we created the acronym for G.R.A.C.E. Ministries— Greater Roseburg Area Committee for Evangelism.

It was through G.R.A.C.E. that I discovered my God-given gifts, one of which was creativity, and often times I needed to be reminded in those early days of G.R.A.C.E. to not get ahead of God.

When I'd get ready to leave, after meeting with Ruth, she would lovingly remind me, "Sue, God is never in a hurry, and remember to bathe everything you do in prayer. A scripture that I heard on numerous occasions was, *"But seek first the kingdom of God and His righteousness, and all these things shall be added to you. Therefore do not worry about tomorrow, for tomorrow will worry about its own things. Sufficient for the day is its own trouble." Matthew 6:33-34 NKJV.*

The committee prayed for six months before the first conference.

In the beginning years of serving on the G.R.A.C.E. Ministries team, I used to judge myself based on how I looked, behaved or felt. If I liked what I saw in the mirror, I felt more worthy of Gods love for me, or when things went smoothly and my performance seemed adequate, I felt I was loved more by God.

When I felt discouraged, I would look inward so I could try to correct what was wrong, instead of fixing my eyes on Jesus the Author and finisher of my faith. The G.R.A.C.E. team and the speakers helped me realize the importance for spending time in the Word and prayer. That I needed to be a woman in the Word daily to have Him be reflected in my life so He could give me my marching orders for my life and for the planning of G.R.A.C.E. I have come a long way in my spiritual journey so far and still have more traveling to do with Him. But now I am finding joy in the journey.

When I came on board, Ruth still owned the bookstore—so I was her hands and feet. She trusted me to do what needed to be done. I also learned to notice the fruit in other women's lives and so wanted that for my life. She also taught me how to evaluate speakers— to find speakers who could reach today's women. She gave me books and tapes to listen and read. I was hungry to learn. It only took one person to believe in me to get my fire started.

In April of 1997 I spoke at a women's retreat for Riverside Community Church of God in Cottage Grove, Oregon. I received a call from the women's ministry director from Riverside Church asking me to be the speaker for their upcoming retreat. I told her I was not a speaker and she needed to go back to the committee and share that with them. A week later she called and said, "It's unanimous. We're sure we want you." I got really weak in the knees as I hung up the phone. I dropped to my knees and began to pray, asking God to empower me with a message that would speak to the hearts of the women attending. It was the beginning of praying for the attendees, and that prayer continues today. I was desperate for the Lord to give me a message. I remember one of our speakers from G.R.A.C.E. having a book on public speaking; so I purchased the book, *Speak up with Confidence* by Carol Kent. I devoured the book to find out how to make an outline and I still refer to Carol's teaching today. I remember returning from the retreat sharing with Ruth the power of the prayers that were prayed and how the Holy Spirit anointed me and showed up and moved in a powerful way in the hearts of the women. I told her about my desire to pursue speaking. She replied in her gentle way, "God is not in a hurry Sue, and if He wants you to have a speaking ministry, it will still be there when your kids are grown. The most important thing you can do for God is to be the best mother you can be. God has entrusted you to raise your sons. If God has a speaking ministry for you, it will still be there when your boys are grown. Remember God is never in a hurry."

Well, I was expecting Ruth to get all excited about my speaking and I'll have to admit that her advice was not what I was looking for. Disappointed? Yes. But I trusted and respected her and her advice, so my focus changed to— Lord your kingdom come your will be done. Lord, I do not want to make anything happen. Just as the earth revolves around the sun, I want my life to revolve around you. I want you as my absolute center and I never want to get ahead of you.

I learned from Ruth as she ingrained in me that nothing moves, exists or has its being unless God has ordained it. I desired to know the same God she so passionately knew, served and talked about. Ruth and other faithful Christian women were a passage for me— getting me from one place to another in my spiritual walk. My desire is to help women and be a passage for them. I never wanted to be a dead-end. I wanted to pass on what I had learned when I reached a destination in my spiritual walk. I wanted to help others get there. Like a tour guide giving them the best information and resources to make their passage from one place to the next with confidence in the One whom they are seeking. My passion along the way is to encourage and inspire them to the purpose and plan that God has for them. Through G.R.A.C.E. Ministries I realized I could have many mentors; I listened to gifted speakers, read their books and applied the truths from them.

I am so thankful for the opportunity to have had the godly influence of so many gifted women during the ten years I served with the G.R.A.C.E. Ministries team. My journey begins new every day spending time with Him in His Word and prayer.

"I beseech you therefore, brethren, by the mercies of God, to present your bodies a living sacrifice, holy, acceptable to God, which is your spiritual service. And be not fashioned according to this world; but be ye transformed by the renewing of your mind, and ye may prove what is good and acceptable and perfect will of God." Romans 12:1-2 ASV.

My desire is to be a woman of the Word who walks by faith and not by sight to do His Kingdom work.

G.R.A.C.E. Ministries was Ruth's vision. She also had the wisdom of the Word and shared it with others. We were united in prayer and kept G.R.A.C.E. Ministries interdenominational (or vanilla). Because we sought to be interdenominational, our conferences were always held at a different church each year. Through time spent in the Word and prayer I learned how to approach pastors of other denominations, form relationships and assure them that we were not a threat to their congregations. This has carried over into the community I live in now. God has interesting ways of training you for the plans He has for you.

G.R.A.C.E. Ministries is where I was mentored, grew and learned. *"Remember those who led you, who spoke the word of God to you, and considering the result of their conduct, imitate their faith." Hebrews 13:7 NASB.* I was drawn by their faith and the fruit I saw from their lives and wanted to follow their example. Therefore, I felt ready and was excited to take up the reins of leadership of G.R.A.C.E. Ministries when Ruth retired, and I did for a time, but God had a different plan for my life.

My prayer at the altar all those Sundays for my husband's salvation was answered in a big way. Not only his salvation, but he became a pastor! When Rick accepted a senior pastor position in another part of Oregon and we moved to Cottage Grove, I grieved for the women and ministry I loved and was committed to. Rick assured me that God was not just moving him but that He had a plan for me. I waited and listened for God to lead me.

I didn't have the hope of Jesus Christ growing up or in my early adulthood so I spent too much time focusing on the past letting it mold me. This is why I am passionate to encourage and enlighten women about the purpose and plan

God has for them, and to give women the desire to know God's heart as well as for women to feel valued, to equip them to rise above their circumstances and to be totally devoted to God. I made myself available to God and He led me to other women to help them find that hope. God wants women to know that there is hope— things don't always have to be the way they are. There are so many women in different seasons of their lives—stay-at-home moms, working women, retired women and widows. They didn't know the love of the Lord nor how much he values them.

I prayed asking God to show me how to use what He had developed in me those ten years of internship to help the women of Cottage Grove. Some asked me to bring the G.R.A.C.E. Ministries conference-style program to Cottage Grove, yet I waited until God revealed his plan.

He began to put dedicated women around me from different churches with the same passion I had. We began praying together on a regular basis. We started a community Bible study with ladies from different local churches.

Based on what I learned through G.R.A.C.E. Ministries I organized S.H.E.Z.A.M.—Sisters Humbly Excited about the Master. S.H.E.Z.A.M. Ministry was a non-profit organization through Riverside Community Church of God in

Cottage Grove, Oregon, for ten years. Working with other churches in the community, it provided an annual inspirational women's conference, open to all women and free of charge. It's mission was to encourage and enlighten women about the purpose and plan God had for them, and to give women the desire to know God's heart as well as for women to feel valued, to equip them to rise above their circumstances and to be totally devoted to God.

Like the fruit of the G.R.A.C.E. Ministries conferences, women became excited about serving the Lord and their churches became healthier because of the conference and what God did. God blessed S.H.E.Z.A.M. We grew so large that we had to start holding the conference at the local high school.

Much prayer, much blessing;
Little prayer, little blessing;
And no prayer, no blessing.

I also credit the success of S.H.E.Z.A.M. to Ruth's mentoring me for many years and to being a part of G.R.A.C.E. Ministries. Ruth's wise counsel to wait and pray has made every ministry opportunity God has allowed me to be involved in bring glory to Him, because of the foundation of prayer that has gone before.

> *"But those who wait on the LORD*
> *Shall renew their strength;*
> *They shall mount up with wings like eagles,*
> *They shall run and not be weary,*
> *They shall walk and not faint." Isaiah 40:31 NKJV.*

Organizing a conference isn't easy. It's hard. There are always difficulties—not enough money, someone wanting it to only be for their denomination—yet the money always comes in, the work gets done, and it continues to be interdenominational (vanilla).

* * *

I'm experiencing a transition of waiting. In 2008 I believed God was telling me to resign from all ministries and my position as Pastor of Women's Ministries at Riverside Community Church of God in Cottage Grove, Oregon. He was speaking to me through His word, *"Cease striving* (Sue) *and, know that I am God;" Psalm 46:10 NASB.*

Through several recurring dreams (which seemed more like nightmares) and Scripture verses rang like warning sirens, I ceased striving. It wasn't easy for me to do. I suffered agony, pain and sorrow and went into a depression leaving the ministry where I learned how to be a loving wife, mother, mentor and women's ministry leader. I believe God has another chapter in my life and more for me to conquer. I have been still before Him and still do not have a clear picture of what is in store for me regarding ministry. But I do know this, while I am in this waiting phase God is still using me as I take my everyday life and place it before Him. Do I get discouraged? I sure do.

God wants me to spend uninterrupted time with Him so He can teach me great and unsearchable things I don't now know yet. So I'm sitting at his feet.

So far the journey has been amazing and astounding. I am humbled, honored and privileged for all that God has and is allowing me to do for Him.

Oswald Chambers said, *"Living a life of faith means never knowing where you are being led. But it does mean loving and knowing the One who is leading."*

I'm finding joy in His journey.

"For we do not preach ourselves but Jesus Christ as Lord, and ourselves as your servants for Jesus' sake. II Corinthians 4:5 NIV.

One Day You Will Lead This Ministry
Roxanne's Story

"Tend the flock of God that is your charge, not by constraint but willingly, not for shameful gain but eagerly, not as domineering over those in your charge but being examples to the flock. And when the chief Shepherd is manifested you will obtain the unfading crown of glory. . . . Clothe yourselves, all of you, with humility toward one another, for 'God opposes the proud, but gives grace to the humble.' Humble yourselves therefore under the mighty hand of God, that in due time he may exalt you. Cast all your anxieties on him, for he cares about you." I Peter 5:2-7 RSV.

At the time I became involved with G.R.A.C.E. Ministries, I was fifty years old, divorced with three grown children and two grandchildren. To summarize those fifty years – the first thirty were spent serving self and for the next twenty years learning to serve God. I was thirty when I rededicated my life to Christ.

My oldest sister died less than a year after she was diagnosed with terminal cancer. Her death was a huge loss for me and my family. The reality of death, brought to my front door, made me evaluate my own life. It was in my search to gain understanding and answers that I met and fell in love with Jesus Christ. Even though I had accepted Jesus as a child, I had not developed a personal relationship with Him.

After my recommitment, life became new and exciting. I enjoyed several years of getting acquainted with God and witnessed His power at work in my life many times. Then I experienced a trial that really tested my faith. In fact, it almost broke it. I went through a horrible divorce. I didn't recognize it, but looking back I can see I was disappointed in God and maybe angry with Him because he didn't fix my marriage and I began to harbor a rebellious heart. So for several seasons I tested him and the more I tested, the dryer the seasons became until I found myself in a miserable place, a desert without refreshment of any kind. But he remained faithful, and firm. Thankfully, He didn't give me what I deserved nor did he give me what I was seeking. He had a better plan. *"For I know the plans I have for you says the Lord, plans for welfare and not for evil, to give you a future and a hope." Jeremiah 29:11 RSV.*

I don't recall how I heard about G.R.A.C.E. Ministries. I do remember the first conference I attended was at the Nazarene Church and the speaker was Evelyn Christenson. She inspired me to find prayer partners to pray with which eventually led me to two ladies I met while attending the Nazarene Church. They have been a major influence in my life. I can't begin to tell how valuable and precious they are but I encourage anyone who is trying to travel this road alone, to find someone to pray with. I think I attended every conference after that first one. Then in 1998 I attended my first recruitment meeting for an upcoming conference and that changed my course.

Several years after my divorce, and while attending the Nazarene Church, I was still trying to recover from my desert journey. During one of the services I heard about a recruitment meeting for G.R.A.C.E. Ministries. I invited a couple of friends and co-workers to go with me, and we attended the meeting where Andrea Minor was speaking. I don't even remember what she was saying. I think she was sharing how she became involved in G.R.A.C.E and she was taking Sue

Haberly's place as leader. Out of the blue, this small voice said "One day you will be leading this ministry." I remember feeling embarrassed that I would even think that and I wondered what my friends sitting next to me would think if they knew my thoughts. I tried to focus on the speaker but again that same voice came back a couple of more times and I finally said, "Lord, if this is you, I want to do what you ask, but I feel so unworthy and inadequate that I'm not sure it is really you. But if it is you, and if this should come to pass, they need to pursue me, then I will know it is from you and I will do it." I felt pretty safe with that because there wasn't even a position available; the position had been filled by Andrea. And what were the odds they would ever contact me, if it did come open? They didn't even know who I was. I quickly dismissed the idea.

I don't remember the details, but I do remember receiving a call at work from Andrea a few weeks after that meeting. She was looking for one of my friends who had attended the meeting, but for some reason she had asked for or was given me. In the course of the conversation, she invited me, along with the co-workers who had attended the recruitment meeting, to a prayer meeting at her home to pray for the upcoming conference. It was at that meeting she shared news that her husband was being transferred to the East Coast and this would be her last conference. They weren't announcing the position but they were looking for a new director. I thought I saw a look on her face when she said "looking for a new director," as if to say she knew she was talking to that person. But it appeared she was looking at the person sitting next to me and she well may have been. I wasn't connecting the dots or my conversation with God. I was just feeling disappointed that Andrea would be leaving after the conference. I attended the conference that year and thoroughly enjoyed the speaker, Sylvia Harney. I never gave another thought to God's still small voice or the idea of leadership.

It had to be God inspired when Sue passed the gavel to me. I was an unlikely candidate for the job. I never felt I had anything to offer and didn't have any real gifts or talents. I wasn't confident enough to do much of anything for fear of failing. I remember, as a young Christian, sharing that with my Mom and she told me the best gift I could give was love. She said, "Pray and ask God for the gift of love." As I began to pray, I not only started feeling love but I also began to have a great burden for others. I would spend hours daily in prayer for my family and friends and for people I didn't even know. Looking back, that was some of the preparation needed for this ministry. Interestingly, as I read some of Ruth's excerpts for this book, I realized that my prayer time was happening at the same time she was starting G.R.A.C.E. Ministries!

* * *

A few months after the conference, Sue Haberly called me and asked if I would be interested in co-hosting the director's position with another lady. I felt comfortable knowing I had someone else to share the duties and by this time I was ready to start getting involved somewhere. So I accepted to co-host but before I had a chance to meet the other person, Sue called and said she had changed her mind, due to some other obligations. "Would you consider taking it?" Sue asked. I told her I would pray about it and let her know when I came up to S.H.E.Z.A.M. The S.H.E.Z.A.M. conference was still a couple of months out and that would give me time to pray about it.

I was scared to death and feeling very inadequate and unworthy. Could I do it? I was not equipped to take on something like this. What if I accepted and failed? I prayed and prayed. On one hand, because of my burden for the lost, I wanted to do it, but the fears were so overwhelming that I didn't believe I could do it. As S.H.E.Z.A.M. drew closer, I was getting more anxious knowing that I had to give Sue an answer soon. I was really praying. One day I was talking to God, actually I was begging Him for some direction. And it was like a curtain pulled back, revealing the conversation I'd had with him at that recruitment meeting. It was like a huge weight removed and I knew I was to accept it. I said, "Okay, Lord, I'll do it even though I have no talents and I can't even speak! He said, "I know you can't do it, but I can." *"With man this is impossible, but with God all things are possible." Matthew 19:26 RSV.*

After accepting the position I drove to Cottage Grove a few times to visit with Sue. She offered so much support as I struggled with being adequate enough to lead this ministry. She prayed for me, encouraged me and shared information on G.R.A.C.E. and ministry work in general. She taught me how to put on a conference. Some of her advice has proved to be invaluable and later on saved us a lot of trouble. Two things that really stick out in my mind are "Stay Vanilla" and "Seek God Continually". She said we would have all different kinds of religions, personalities and backgrounds at the conferences and each with a different idea, belief or opinion. It would be best to "Stay Vanilla". Keep a sweet fragrance and be neutral, staying away from controversies that could cause division and strife. I think that has also helped keep the G.R.A.C.E. Board in unity. Even when in disagreement we operate in unity. And this could also be due to the fact that we "Seek God continually".

* * *

One unforgettable answer to prayer was when we were praying for 300 Bibles to be provided for the conference. Our prayer chairman at that time felt that was what we needed to do. I don't even remember how we came up with that number. Maybe that was how many we expected to attend that year. We didn't share it with anyone but God. We didn't know it but at the same time we were praying, our speaker that year, was prompted to bring Bibles to the conference. She didn't say anything to us but she put out a request via email and this man she didn't know responded. This person who donated them had no knowledge of our prayer request either. He donated exactly 300 Bibles!

Another memory is of a woman who came forward at one of the altar calls. She patiently waited for someone to pray with her but everyone was busy praying with someone else. I finally went up only because she was standing there so long and I felt sorry for her. I also felt a certain obligation as the leader. But the truth was I was afraid if I prayed with her, she would be short changed by my puny sounding prayers when we had powerful prayer warriors there to pray with her. So I decided to go up and tell her someone would be with her in a minute and just stand there with her until someone was available. When I reached her, she assumed I was going to pray for her and she started telling me she needed a healing for her back. I didn't have the heart to tell her that someone would pray for her shortly. So I began to pray, but my words felt empty and inadequate. Once again I decided I would ask her to wait for someone else to pray for her. All of a sudden she started bending over touching her toes and jumping up and down and saying she was healed! I was awestruck as I witnessed God's power and answered prayer in both our lives. When we are weak and feel inadequate, God is strong.

Other stories of how people's lives were changed through God's power at G.R.A.C.E. Ministries conferences are recorded in Part II of this book.

* * *

At first G.R.A.C.E. Ministries was an annual women's Christian conference held on a weekend. Later while praying over the prayer requests that were submitted at the conference, we saw the great needs of the women. We wanted something to address the issues where women were struggling and equip them with tools to improve their situations and draw them into a new or closer relationship with God. Workshops were developed. While the conference addresses a general audience, the workshops focus on specific issues.

The conferences and workshops allow contact twice a year, but what about the other 363 days of the year? From the altar calls, prayer requests and talking with the women we saw a great need for Christian counseling that didn't involve a cost. We know the solutions to these women's problems are in the Bible, if they would pick it up and read it. Some of these women were right where we had come from and we had experienced victory through Jesus by using biblical principles. We wanted to share that knowledge, support, encourage and pray for them.

* * *

I would describe my leadership as a servant, behind the scenes, encouraging others in their God-given gifts to serve the hurting women in Douglas County and surrounding areas.

Ruth Fowler, Roxanne Laurance and Sue Haberly

G.R.A.C.E. G.U.Y.S.
Our Story
By Brian

I became involved with G.R.A.C.E. Ministries some time ago. I did whatever was needed. My wife, Robin, would ask, "Honey, will you take out the trash." Or, "Honey, we need some tables moved."

Later it wasn't Robin asking, it was a voice from the Lord, "I want you to serve the ladies."

Confused, I answered, "I thought I was, Lord."

"I want you to serve a meal to the ladies."

I couldn't imagine how I was going to do that. Like many of the testimonies recorded in this book, what we can't do, God can. God opens doors for opportunities. He hooked me up with Tom Booth from Roseburg Christian Fellowship (RCF). Tom served as a 1st sergeant in the military and had experience cooking and serving hundreds in a timely fashion.

Thus G.R.A.C.E. G.U.Y.S. was organized as an off-shoot of G.R.A.C.E. Ministries. God wanted all the ladies to hear the speaker instead of being in the kitchen preparing meals.

G.R.A.C.E. G.U.Y.S. is made up partly of husbands of the women serving in G.R.A.C.E. Ministries. It snowballed. We have thirteen men meeting regularly. We like to help out.

Like G.R.A.C.E. is an acrostic of Greater Roseburg Area Committee for Evangelism, G.R.A.C.E. G.U.Y.S. represents Guys United Yeshua Service. (Yeshua in Hebrew, was a common name among Jews of the Second Temple Period, and is thought by some scholars and religious groups to be the Hebrew or Aramaic name for Jesus.)

We wear white chef coats with our insignia on the back. My brother, Kevin, and a co-worker, Ron Mentzer, designed the logo for G.R.A.C.E. G.U.Y.S., after several sketches, for the back of the coat. On the front of our jackets are the names of the many different churches we represent throughout Douglas County, Oregon.

G.R.A.C.E. Ministries gives us a budget and we aim to be good stewards of it. As well as the budget, we go into the community seeking donations so there won't be an extra burden on G.R.A.C.E. Ministries. Some businesses give each year; others are unable to donate because of hard times.

G.R.A.C.E. G.U.Y.S. is made up of men from diverse backgrounds, many with service related occupations in the community. Some are retired or semi retired, with experience in the military, forestry, and law enforcement, as well as other fields.

We're here to serve. It's all about our Heavenly Father, and we're all serving the same God. We're brothers and sisters in the Lord.

Humble and appreciative, G.R.A.C.E. G.U.Y.S. have a blast while serving others. They're even available to assist other groups, family reunions and events.

G.R.A.C.E. G.U.Y.S.

Part II

In Memory of LaDonna
1936 to 2001

By her daughter, Jennifer

I was a young married during the early years of G.R.A.C.E. Ministries. My mother thought there ought to be a women's spiritual enrichment in Roseburg. At that time there weren't conferences for women like Women of Faith or Beth Moore. Many women in the Roseburg area suffered from abuse and low self-esteem. The goal of G.R.A.C.E. Ministries was to enrich women's lives.

Women needed to be blessed and uplifted. G.R.A.C.E. Ministries offered powerful speakers and great worship for Christians and non-Christians. Many women found a church home after attending a G.R.A.C.E Ministries conference.

My mother grew up in a strong Christian home and accepted the Lord as her Savior as a child. She had a servant's heart and was gifted at working behind the scenes.

Lois' Story

It was a breath of fresh air to me when G.R.A.C.E. Ministries started because the churches needed to be doing things together and whom better than the ladies to lead it. I think it is one of the best things that ever happened and is happening in Roseburg.

I remember the emphasis on prayer and a prayer team and having representatives from all cooperating churches doing the planning. I love the fact that they moved from church to church for hosting the events. It gave a sense of being involved in the community.

I believe it was a life changing experience to many women. I personally appreciated being able to invite friends to an inspirational Christian women's social event where they were pampered.

Sherry's Story

Several years ago, a radio advertisement introduced me to G.R.A.C.E. Ministries

That year the conference was held in Winston, Oregon, so I decided to go, never suspecting how my life would be affected.

At my first conference, during the freewill offering, they mentioned they were in need of postage stamps. They asked if any of us had stamps in our purses and wanted to donate them to drop them in the offering. I had a few, so I gladly put them in. After the conference was over, I decided that if they needed stamps, I would send them more. I mailed the stamps along with a thank you note, probably in the form of a poem, because that is what I often did. To my surprise I received a phone call from Jan Findlay. She introduced herself as being part of the G.R.A.C.E. team and thanked me for the stamps and note. She said she'd like to meet me and invited me over to her house for tea. She said, "When we opened your letter, we said, we need to meet this girl!" I met with Jan and decided I liked the heart of G.R.A.C.E. These were women of faith who prayed and believed God to supply every single need for every conference and He never let them down. *That made my heart happy and my heart loooooooves to be happy!*

I'm an encourager, so I began to bless the ministry with notes, poems, gift baskets, etc. After Sue Haberly stepped down and moved to Cottage Grove, I continued to send her notes for a long while. Roxanne Laurance took on the leadership and I worked quite a bit with her doing all the above, plus graphic posters, flyers, etc. I also encouraged my church and our women's ministry to donate time and money for needed supply expenses and any other thing we could do to help, especially the first year they held the conference at our church, Garden Valley Christian Assembly.

One year I created graphic-designed laminated bookmarks with scriptures and my poems to give to every woman that came. Another year, I created a small folder with pamphlets from many ministries around Douglas County that the women might be interested in blessing or being blessed by. I've played the piano at a few conferences, made speaker gift baskets, even decorated a welcome room for one of the speakers. (I may have overwhelmed her with all the ribbon streamers in the shower, scripture cards on the inside toilet lid, sparkly confetti, roses and goodies all over the room!) And I even recommended a few names of possible speakers to pray about. I did what I could to be a blessing.

I enjoyed my time serving with G.R.A.C.E., but had to step down when family medical needs required my time and attention. G.R.A.C.E. came into a time of change too. It's not a once-a-year conference anymore. They are branching out into workshop seminars and connecting women with prayer partners, etc., but the heart of G.R.A.C.E. is still the same, they love the women of Douglas County and want them to know the Father who loves them and who can change their lives for the better, the God who can supply every need when approached with faith and prayer.

My life has been enriched by G.R.A.C.E. Ministries. The faith and prayer I encountered fanned a spark in me that gets passed on every time I give.

Pat's Story

Some people call me the "funny lady of G.R.A.C.E. Ministries." Let me tell you how this came about. I was born in 1935. Oh, that's too far back.

About ten years ago Roxanne asked me if I would be interested in being involved in G.R.A.C.E. Ministries. She explained how God had called her to lead the conference, but she needed someone to be the emcee. So we joked about me being Aaron to her Moses.

I always wanted to be involved in G.R.A.C.E., but it had never worked out. I thought I could help with being on one of the committees or the board; I was really surprised when she asked me to be the emcee. I told her I would pray about it, but I knew the answer already because I felt in my spirit that God was in this and He was calling me to some new and exciting ministry.

I prayed about it to make sure this was really God speaking and not me wanting to do something for God. For many years I had a burden for women and had been teaching women's Bible studies. After I said I would help out, I realized that I had never done anything like it before, but Roxanne and another friend thought I could do it. God also assured me that I was His workmanship and He would equip me with every good work. He would be my strength and guide. He gives me His great love and His grace is sufficient.

For some wonderful reason known only to God when I get up in front of the women, the spirit of joy comes over me. The spirit of joy of the Lord also seems to come over everyone there and God gives me funny things to say. I'm somewhat prepared with what I'm going to say, but most of the funny things come out spontaneously by what is happening or what someone else has just said.

What a wonderful group of godly women I have worked with in this ministry. The foundation of G.R.A.C.E. Ministries is based on Jesus Christ, leading women to salvation and to grow in the Lord. All that we do is saturated in prayer.

Diane's Story

It was 1998 and I was working at the Sun Studs office with Roxanne Laurance. Roxanne had asked me to join her at the annual G.R.A.C.E. Ministries conference in prior years, but I always had something that conflicted. When she asked me to go with her to the 1998 conference being held at the Baptist Church in downtown Roseburg, I agreed to commit to going on Friday night only, as I had a long list of errands which I planned to do on Saturday.

The speaker that year was Lori Salierno. She combined her wisdom of the scriptures and her life experiences traveling on missions and being with Mother Theresa and working with the under-privileged, and did it in a way that touched my spirit immensely. I remember laughing and crying and sometimes doing both at the same time.

I also remember writing down lots of good "nuggets" from her wealth of wisdom of Jesus and her walk with Him. The experience Friday night was so wonderful and overwhelming to me that I remember saying goodbye to my "to do" list so that I could be there to listen to whatever Lori had in store for me on Saturday. The worship time was also fantastic.

I saw a teacher my husband worked with at the Saturday session and she had just been told her Mom was diagnosed with cancer. I'll never forget the tears we shared that day standing in the church. Her Mom lost her battle and passed away a year or so later, but the heartfelt time we spent talking about the news and about her Mom will stay with me forever. It brings me to tears just recalling the moment again now.

There's just something about being in God's house that puts a greater spirit of compassion into the heart. This is the reason it is so important for me as a Christian to attend church and be with God and the spirit that dwells within the church and the congregation. Thank you for this opportunity to share my story, and God Bless Ruth Fowler for her dedication and energy to bringing women in Douglas County to the light of Gods unconditional love, compassion, and guidance.

Madge's Story

Ruth and I attended church and Bible study together. As she prayed about her vision, I became excited and joined her in prayer. Finally the first conference came and I attended, and continued to attend the conferences for about seven years. When my mother-in-law needed care, she became my priority and I took a break. After she passed away, I volunteered to help in G.R.A.C.E. Ministries.

I've enjoyed all the speakers and look forward to the conferences. I've also enjoyed everyone involved in G.R.A.C.E. and look forward to our meetings and the prayer time.

Robin's Story

I had a wonderful little grandma who took my sister and me to church, Vacation Bible School and invited us to spend the night, often. She read the Bible to us, prayed with us and taught us how to memorize Bible verses. She prayed for God to give us the right husbands. We were little and we thought she was a little kooky, but I have that wonderful husband, Brian, that she prayed for. I now understand the value of her prayers. She prayed for our family until the very end. She was a wonderful example of how to live a godly life. This is how I came to know the Lord.

When I got a job at Sun Studs I became friends with Roxanne Laurence, who has become my precious friend and sister in Christ. She invited me to go to a meeting for G.R.A.C.E. Ministries where they were recruiting helpers. I questioned what I could do— I can't sing. I'm not an eloquent speaker. I felt inadequate before the Lord, not knowing what my talent was. I went to Him in prayer and asked, "How can I serve you, Lord? I don't have much to offer you." I felt like He told me to serve him by serving others. *"'for I was hungry, and ye gave me to eat; I was thirsty, and ye gave me drink; I was a stranger, and ye took me in; naked, and ye clothed me; I was sick, and ye visited me; I was in prison, and ye came unto me. And the King shall answer and say unto them, Verily I say unto you, Inasmuch as ye did it unto one of these my brethren, even these least, ye did it unto me.'" Matthew 25:35-36, 40 ASV.*

I became one of the hostesses and have been the committee leader for several years as well. We greet the ladies as they come in the door with hugs and hand shakes. This is a time to set "me" aside and be God's hands and feet. That is what God has called me to do for Him.

My husband is the leader of G.R.A.C.E. G.U.Y.S. He's met some great men through this ministry. (Some of them are Christians and others are not.) They serve side by side building relationships and witnessing. I know that they have been blessed by it. I see first hand how these men have blessed the women and they are being blessed in return.

As a little girl I thought my grandmother was a little kooky, now I know better. God blessed me with a grandmother like Timothy of the Bible – *"For I am mindful of the sincere faith within you, which first dwelt in your grandmother Lois and your mother Eunice, and I am sure that it is in you as well." II Timothy 1:5 NASB.*

Vicki's Story

The first time I heard about G.R.A.C.E. Ministries was from Roxanne. We'd worked together for many years. She was a good friend and we always ragged on each other. I'd call her a holy-roller and she'd say things like, "God told me He's going to get you."

When Sue moved to Cottage Grove, G.R.A.C.E. Ministries was put on hold for a short time. During that period the women in Douglas County were hungry for a conference so a bunch of us would drive to Cottage Grove to attend S.H.E.Z.A.M. where we heard wonderful speakers that inspired us. I only went because Roxanne invited me to go.

It was when Roxanne took on the leadership of the conference that I stepped in to help her out. She needed help and I'd do anything I could, except pray, for my friend. It was at the first conference, after G.R.A.C.E. Ministries resumed, that I was saved.

During the conference there was an altar call and women were praying. Out of respect, I bowed my head in the dimly lit room. That's when I felt two hands push me forward. I looked behind me to see the women praying, not pushing me. I didn't know what was happening and it scared the daylights out of me. I found myself walking up front where others were praying. I was confused. I thought what is happening? Am I crazy? It was so unreal.

One of the prayers asked me, "What can I pray with you?"

"I don't know." Confused, finally I said, "Let's pray for my husband."

I felt emptied out and a warm feeling came over me. I also felt goose-bumps.

Afterward, I knew I'd changed, but I didn't understand it, and I was scared to death to tell anybody. So I kept my experience inside until the next conference when I was asked to tell what had happened to me at the conference the previous year.

I think I always believed in God, but I feel a peace now, and a hunger to learn. It isn't always easy, in fact, sometimes it's hard to do. My son and I are Christians. I am patiently waiting for my husband and daughter to see and believe. Although my husband hasn't expressed commitment, he also hasn't closed the door completely – he does tell me to keep praying for him. With that said, I am hopeful that soon we will all be believers. My grandkids like to attend church— so seeds are being sown.

God's Word helps me each day. *"Be still, and know that I am God . . ." Psalms 46:10 RSV.*

I don't know how many women have been saved at a G.R.A.C.E. Ministries conference or others (family members, friends, and co-workers) as a result of changed lives after attending one of the conferences. All I know is that the conference is where I found the Lord and began to walk with Him.

Before G.R.A.C.E. Ministries I felt like I didn't have anybody. After being saved, God put women in my life who walk through the valley with me, they listen to me. One friend explains it as, "Three cords (two people and the Lord) is a strong hold."

It isn't only the conferences that minister to women. G.R.A.C.E. Ministries also offers Centers where one-on-one mentorship happens. I've mentored several women who suffer from depression. I suffered with depression most of my life, so I understand what they are experiencing. Some of the other areas we mentor are abuse, single parenting, finances, and connecting women to available services.

I'm amazed how prayer is still such a huge part of G.R.A.C.E. Ministries. Not only do we pray throughout the year for the conference, but a month before the conference we schedule weekly prayer times for it.

After each conference we go over the prayer requests from the women who attended and pray for them. The following year those same women tell us what happened in answer to their prayer request.

I know I'm an answer to someone's prayer. Roxanne cared about my salvation and I will ever be grateful. And yes I still rag on her.

Ulla's Story

My story starts almost twenty years ago with the sudden death of my daughter from a blood clot in her lungs. She was only twenty-five years old, married and the mother of a five and a half year old daughter and a two and a half year old son.

Having been brought up in the Catholic Church, my other daughter and I went to see the priest of our local church. He said a thirty second prayer and left us standing there. I was devastated. I needed comfort, some kind words, something.

That evening my sister-in-law offered to have her pastor come and talk with us. Pastor Paul came the next day and immediately I felt a connection with him. He was the kindest and most loving person I have ever met, and I knew that he was a man of God. I started going to church every week and I felt he was speaking directly to me in every one of his messages, and I believed what he said.

I became involved with G.R.A.C.E. Ministries through Sue Haberly. She asked me to be the treasurer. So I accepted the responsibility and enjoyed helping in that way. But not all was going well with me.

I was angry with God and I couldn't get rid of my anger for the longest time, not until I realized how much I needed the Lord and that only he could help me. I discovered this while I was on a mission trip to Brazil and only two people know about what happened, until now.

A couple of days before we were to return to the US, we went swimming in the ocean and I got separated from the group and swam out too far. The water was very warm and I was exhausted. I was scared because I knew I couldn't make it back without help and no one was around. I cried out to God and asked Him to help me. I know without a doubt that He was the one who helped me make it back to shore.

I still cry sometimes when I think of my daughter, and I often wonder why she had to die. God's Word says, *"We know that in everything God works for good with those who love him, who are called according to his purpose." Romans 8:28 RSV.*

If I had not gone through the experienced of my daughter's death, I probably wouldn't be attending church, going on mission trips, helping others or involved in G.R.A.C.E. Ministries. I would just be living without knowing first hand that God loves me.

I've met so many women through G.R.A.C.E. who have struggled through their own experiences and have found happiness. There are days when I still struggle, but I know where my help comes from and I feel safe in the shadow of His wings. *"Let me dwell in thy tent for ever! Oh to be safe under the shelter of thy wings!" Psalms 61:4 RSV.*

Jane's Story

I had heard of G.R.A.C.E. Ministries for many years as a member of Hucrest Community Church of God. I have to admit, though, I didn't attend any of the events. In my mind, G.R.A.C.E. wasn't geared for a young wife and mother like me; it was for a different population of women. How wrong I was! When the Reverend Rick Haberly was called to Hucrest as our youth pastor, his lovely wife, Sue, asked me to consider joining the ministry team of G.R.A.C.E. At that time, Ruth Evans, Sandra Weaver, and Jan Findlay, were also on the ministry team.

What I found in these women were sisters who were completely "sold out" for Jesus, humble servants, committed to prayer, and possessed a faith I had not seen in many others. What a wonderful example to a young wife and mother like me. I grew in my faith, my love for others and in service to God.

Just gathering for prayer during organizational meetings was conference enough for me! Yet, at the conferences, I was touched and overwhelmed by the women in attendance. Women from all walks of life and socioeconomic backgrounds came together to worship Jesus, fellowship with other women, be encouraged, and become better followers and servants of the Most Holy!

I will always cherish my time spent serving on G.R.A.C.E. Ministries and can honestly say it was a privilege to serve with such amazing and wonderful women of God.

Shirley J's Story

An appropriate title for my story could be *Shirley's Journey from Hell to Heaven.*

I grew up in a home with a mean, alcoholic, abusive father. From an early age I was abused physically, verbally and mentally by him and at the age of ten I was abused sexually by a family member.

My mother left my father and became a single mom raising four kids. It was the 1960's and, at that time in history, my siblings and I felt a certain stigma being raised in a single parent home. We felt we weren't good enough and it seemed like it was easier being accepted into the wrong crowd. So as a teenager I hung out with them.

When I moved to a new town and didn't know anyone, I was invited to a party to meet some new friends. That night I was drugged and raped. When I became conscious, I was being chocked and beaten. My clothes had been removed and replaced by what I would consider repulsive lingerie. I begged for my life and screamed for help, but no one rescued me. Afterwards, as I drug myself to the bathroom I saw the woman that had invited me to the party. She was in bed with her boyfriend. "Why didn't you help me?" She answered, "You liked it." Because I had a daughter out of wedlock, she reasoned that I asked for it.

Sometime later I went to a bar with a gun. In the booth next to me I recognized the voices of my rapist and the women who had invited me to that party. I'll never forget their conversation. He said, "Get me a women like the last one. It was powerful to have her beg for her life." She replied, "This time it won't cost you fifty dollars, but a hundred."

Enraged, I realized my rapist had paid the woman to get me to the party. I pulled out the gun, but before I could fire it I was tackled by others.

I tried to press charges, but merchant seamen have immunity – so he was protected. Who knows how many women he's raped, and never been prosecuted for his crimes?

It was then that I moved away and buried the rape so deeply in my mind that it would be years later that the memory resurfaced. My brain protected me for many years from reliving that horrific night.

After the rape I started doing drugs and I continued to drink and pick the wrong friends. My boyfriend sexually abused my ten year old daughter, which I didn't know about until years later. When I asked her why she was so upset when I left him? She said, "I thought that's what daddy's did."

The time I took acid I was changing the stations on the radio and I heard a voice. "Who are you?" I asked. The answer came, "Its God. I gave my Son for you. Leave this place." A phone number appeared on the wall. It was the phone number for a drug help line in Denver, Colorado. I called it and they helped me through the acid trip. I never took acid again and I moved to the Oregon coast. I feel such peace there and the coast seems to draw me.

* * *

As a child I always went to Sunday school. Later, I stopped going to church, but I never stopped praying. Like other abuse victims I felt shame, self-loathing and unworthy of love, yet one day while driving over a hundred miles an hour on the freeway, I prayed, "God, when are you going to send someone to love me?"

I'd always looked for love in all the wrong places. A few months later, God sent a kind, caring, compassionate man into my life. I told him everything I had done – the drinking, drugs – everything except the rape, because at that time I didn't remember it. He accepted me and continues to love me all these years later. Because the rape was buried in my memory, I couldn't understand my anger or why I couldn't enjoy an intimate relationship with my husband.

* * *

Roxanne and I have been friends since grade school and about seven years ago she invited me to a G.R.A.C.E. Ministries conference. It was the year Becky Freeman spoke. At the time I was at my wits end. My granddaughter was into drugs. I walked forward at the conference and put the prayer request in for my granddaughter. God answered my prayer. My granddaughter is drug free, has a little boy and is getting married.

It wasn't only my granddaughter that needed God to change her. As I walked forward for prayer, I felt confused. That's when the memory of the rape erupted from the depths.

I knew I needed to let go and let God. I needed to forgive my rapist.

It's been a difficult road. My whole life I felt a battle going on between Satan and God. During the struggle I believe God was fighting for me. In some ways I felt like Job of the Bible. *"And the Lord said to Satan, 'Behold, he is in your power; only spare his life.'" Job 2:6 RSV.* After the rape, I was never validated. I was considered a willing participant. I'd been mistreated by men and even the woman who sold me to my rapist, so I didn't trust men or women.

I've had a lot of yo-yo experiences in my life. While I was being raped, I prayed for my life. After the rape I asked, "Why didn't you let him kill me?" Another example of my waffling was when Roxanne encouraged me over and over again that I needed to find a church family. The Sunday I decided to go church I set the alarm for six thirty – giving myself plenty of time to get ready, and plenty of time to talk myself out of going. I paced. I still wasn't sure. I took a shower, just in case I decided to go. I paced some more. I grabbed my Bible and read. I don't remember the exact verse, but it was something like, *"I have shown you the place you are to go."* I knew God was speaking to me. I went to church that day. I sat in the pew, looked at the picture of Jesus at the front of the sanctuary and felt warm and loved. I reaffirmed my faith and now I'm back in church every Sunday.

I battle depression and suicide and I see a therapist. Because I still have nightmares of the rape, I do take imagery rehearsal therapy (IRT) a medication that's given to veterans who suffer with nightmares from posttraumatic stress disorder (PTSD). But I don't want to take any other drugs, instead I want to rely on God and don't want to mask it, but deal with it.

God is working in my life. With the help of a therapist I've truly forgiven all those who abused me, and I pray more now. The more I pray the more blessing I receive and it isn't always the blessing I expect. I used to be ashamed to pray, because I thought I deserved everything that happened to me and I didn't feel worthy of God's love.

Although I don't know if I'll ever get over my experience, with God's help I'm learning to live with it. I no longer feel revenge, nor do I want to punish them. Maybe those who abused me never experienced God's grace, love and forgiveness.

"'For if ye forgive men their trespasses, your heavenly Father will also forgive you. But if ye forgive not men

their trespasses, neither will your Father forgive your trespasses.'" Matthew 6:14-15 ASV.

My prayer is that my story will touch those who have ever felt like I did – unworthy, used, abused and tossed away. May you find God's grace, love and forgiveness.

Grace, grace, God's grace,
Grace that will pardon and cleanse within;
Grace, grace, God's grace,
Grace that is greater then all our sin!
    Julia H. Johnston

Judy's Story

I wasn't raised in a Christian home. If someone didn't take me to church, I walked to the nearest one in my neighborhood. In my heart I wanted to serve God, but all the women seemed to serve Him by cooking or sewing and I wasn't interested in those things. How could I serve Him when my talent was art?

As a teenager I attended a youth program with some friends, but the adults in that church were critical of teenagers. I was hurt by them and it caused me to stop going to church.

Living in Iowa, as a farmer's wife, I received a devastating blow when my husband told me he didn't want to be married anymore. At thirty I became a single mom with two little girls. I decided to go to Iowa State University to finish my degree in elementary education. I thought I was doing okay, but I was wrong. I was devastated from going through a divorce and rejection and parenting alone. At that time I didn't know how much my Heavenly Father loved me. Without realizing it at the time, God was with me. *"He brought me up out of the pit of destruction, out of the miry clay, and set my feet on the rock making my footsteps firm." Psalm 40:2 NAS.*

Psalm 40 was life changing. God pulled me out of the pit and said I would tell congregations of His goodness to me. I didn't understand how that could be, when I was afraid to speak in front of others.

I was raising my daughters, working and a student at Iowa State University when a friend asked me to go to church with him. He was a Christian and I could see he knew something about Jesus that I didn't. I felt so lost and abandoned that I wanted to find out if this church had some words of encouragement, since I was a single mother and feeling worthless. I listened to some evangelists at the church on the teachings on the gift of the Spirit and how God can wipe our past out and give us new hope for a new beginning. I made my decision to accept Jesus as my Lord and Savior.

The man who invited me to church became my husband and in 1979 we moved to Oregon. We knew Douglas County was where God wanted us. We found a church where we were loved and mentored. I was shy and my pastor's wife had a Bible study at her home that I attended and there were older women who mentored and guided me with love and the Word of God. They would often tell me, "What a woman of God you will be—you'll speak to other women."

After returning from a retreat, I was asked to say a few words in front of my church on a Sunday night. I was scared to death. The Holy Spirit assured me, "If you will get up, I will fill your mouth with my words." It was a good thing, because I was shaking and unable to read my notes. I knew when I came down from the pulpit that I could do anything that God told me to do if I would be obedient to His call.

I was introduced to G.R.A.C.E. Ministries when someone came into the Christian bookstore that I owned and asked me to put a G.R.A.C.E. Conference flyer up. I was very curious about what G.R.A.C.E. Ministries had to offer.

I attended that conference by myself and the speaker, Daisy Hepburn, ministered deeply to my heart and soul. I loved being in a meeting with women and it was a gift from God to me. I no longer felt discouraged or all alone and I knew that God sent G.R.A.C.E. to me and the women of Douglas County. What a blessing and how I longed to be part of G.R.A.C.E.

I am continually growing spiritually. As an intercessor—I love to pray for people. While praying for others, I constantly seek my Heavenly Father asking, *"Lord, if I'm ever off base, please correct me."*

At a G.R.A.C.E. Ministries board meeting I attended, there were sign-up sheets for various committees. One was for a prayer leader to lead the prayer for the conference. I knew I was an intercessor; I'd even attended an intercessor conference. *"But, Lord, I'm not a leader."* God spoke to me, "I've called to you for a long time." I became the prayer leader of G.R.A.C.E.

God has answered many prayers. One year we didn't have a church to hold the conference at. We prayed and a church became available. Another time, when we didn't have very much money, we prayed and I saw a vision of a huge pile of dollar bills in the middle of the circle—like seed money. When I shared my vision with the board they thought we should take an offering of a dollar every week during intercession for the conference. That year we had more than enough money.

There is nothing like G.R.A.C.E Ministries. Getting together with our sisters and seeing women in unity is a dream come true for me. I've had to cut back in areas I've served in the past, but G.R.A.C.E. isn't one of them. I am passionate about G.R.A.C.E. Ministries. I love working and praying with the women from different denominations that are on the G.R.A.C.E. board, who have a heart for the women in Douglas County. It is so exciting seeing it grow—the outreach, workshops, centers and the women who are touched by God's grace through G.R.A.C.E. Ministries.

One of my favorite Scriptures is: *"Blessed be the God and Father of our Lord Jesus Christ, the Father of mercies and God of all comfort, who comforts us in all our affliction so that we will be able to comfort those who are in any affliction with the comfort with which we ourselves are comforted by God." II Corinthians 1:3-4 NAS.*

Shirley K's Story

I've been involved with G.R.A.C.E. Ministries since moving to Roseburg in 2003 so I know first hand how the G.R.A.C.E. Ministries team prays for every part of the conference, including everyone who will be attending, the speaker, those who serve in the different areas and those who lead the music worship. Therefore, I wasn't surprised to be ministered to at the 2010 conference when we sang—

> Let it flow, let it flow
> Let the power of the Holy Ghost take control
> There's a hurricane in the forecast
> And the wind is starting to flow
> It's the power, power, power of the Holy Ghost.

While singing I remembered a true story I'd heard about God's miracle in Israel during the 1973 Yom Kippur (Day of

Atonement) War. Israeli soldiers in the ancient city of Golan were making their way to a nearby village. Suddenly, they found themselves in the middle of a mine field. They began to poke around with their bayonets, trying to find the mines, when a strange wind blew. The wind was so strong that it blew away eighteen inches of dirt, exposing over 1,000 mines. Once the mines were exposed, the wind stopped and the men safely walked across the field.

In 2010 my family was faced with severe problems, which seemed like land mines ready to explode. One morning our Lord spoke to me, *"As I blew the dirt away from the land mines in Israel years ago, I will do so for the land mines you are facing."*

It was while praying with my daughter-in-law that I felt God's spirit and assurance that He would dismantle the problems my family was facing. And He did!

Reminded of how God worked in my family, I was moved during the conference as we sang—*There's a hurricane in the forecast and the wind is starting to blow.*

I thank the prayer team for their prayers, faithfulness and ministry.

Jackie's Story

I was introduced to G.R.A.C.E. Ministries many years ago when my friend, Laura, asked me to join with other women and pray. I was amazed at the dedication and faithfulness of the women who prayed for months for those who would be attending the conference. At that time I had no idea what it was like to put a conference together. That year Pat asked me to pray at the conference. I was shy and my knees were shaking as I stood in front of all those women. Pat held my hand as I prayed and the Lord reminded me of an earlier time when He'd told me I would speak in front of large groups. That was the beginning.

God's plan for me was to share my story with others, yet I was ashamed people wouldn't accept me if they knew what I'd gone through. God used G.R.A.C.E. Ministries to give me the confidence to share His love and plans for me. He's blessed me to bless others.

A Touch of Grace

I was born on a dark stormy night. My dad drove two hundred miles through a Montana blizzard for my birth. Nothing was going to stop him and every time I heard the story I felt like a princess. I felt loved and cherished by both my parents.

Seven years later my life was interrupted by the blare of an ambulance siren and the news that my mom had had a heart attack. That's when I overheard a conversation, "Maybe her last child put a strain on her heart." *It was my fault!* In my little girl mind my mother had risked her life to deliver me! I told no one about the heavy burden I carried. I needed to save her, make things right, give her my heart.

When she returned from the hospital she could no longer climb the stairs and I coped by becoming a good girl, obedient and kind. I was a people pleaser. I received approving nods and pats on the back, yet all the while in the corner of my mind I worried that I wouldn't be able to hold it together.

In the sixth grade I'd describe myself as "a mini ambulance driver." I'd hop on my banana seat bike and peddle as fast as I could with plastic pink streamers on the handlebars flying in the wind. At the downtown pharmacy I loaded up Mom's oxygen tank and returned home panting from the torturous sixteen block ride. I was determined to reach my mother before she ran out of air. Even my best efforts didn't keep the hospital away and soon she was once again in critical care.

I went away to attend college and didn't heed my father's advise. I fell in love with a boy who needed me and I touched the forbidden fruit! A year later I found myself as the Bible puts it, "with child." I needed to maintain my "good girl" statue—so down the isle I went thinking of a white picket fence and pretty flowers all in a row.

Tia's arrival was the essence of squeeze ability! My mom flew out for the big event; the doctor took one look at her eighty-three pounds and immediately admitted her to the hospital. More tears, more surgeries, more guilt!

Two years later my mom was gone and my dad shortly after. (He too had a heart condition.) Death surrounded me. Where were the flowers and the white picket fence?

I became the mom and I didn't even know how to cook! I was living with a violent man driven by the flesh. My family was scattered in different states and even though they were willing to lend a sympathetic ear, I was too afraid to leave my situation. God's Word boomed in my ear. *"If any woman has a husband who is an unbeliever, and he consents to live with her, she should not divorce him."* I Corinthians 7:13 RSV.

Instead I chose "Plan B"—the verbal attack. My manipulation allowed me to unmercifully nag him into conformity. I became well versed in Scripture wars and was able to fire at will any and all condemnation. I also resorted to piously pray, *"Lord either change him or kill him!"* I saw it plain as day—my ten gallon hat was white while my husbands was black as coal—right and wrong.

Very softly, in the middle of my tirade the kind and gentle voice of God whispered, *"Let me handle him child, and allow my focus to be on you."* I knew God was right. He's always right. I stopped kicking and screaming and submitted to His will over my life.

I knew lots of Bible stories, but I never knew God personally. I caught a glimmer of hope—Jesus could be my Savior, and I could take a break! At last, I could live happily ever after! Little did I know that the breaking process was about to be put in motion.

Tia, now joined by her little brothers, became a singing evangelist. She was adept at leading people to Christ. One day she ran through the door yelling, "We need a Bible, quick!" She was about to go through the "Sinners Prayer" with the neighbor girl.

* * *

I accepted an invitation and flew to my nieces wedding in Montana. I took the baby with me and left my two other children with their dad. While I was away, my husband's childhood friend arrived for a visit and changed our lives forever. The friend recently suffered through a horrible divorce and decided to numb the pain with "LSD." He violently smashed through a double paned sliding glass door. In his rampage he was determined to destroy anything in his path. My husband quickly put the children into their room and lifted them through the window as his friend banged mercilessly on the door, finally punching his fist through the door and turning the knob form the inside. My family escaped. The SWAT team arrived in full riot gear and proceeded to kick down my front door, surround my husband's friend and took him into custody. This event caused us to become instant celebrities in the news media and homeless.

.My husband eventually became one of the largest drug dealers in our area. God's angels protected me and my children. We never went without food or shelter. Yet, our nightmare continued as the drug culture closed in on us. The kids and I attended church regularly and put on our happy faces. I was afraid to share what was going on because it would put other lives at risk.

Dangers surrounded us and we were constantly on the move. Living on the street with my three children and pregnant, I was scared and clung to God's Word. *"And we know that God causes all things to work together for good to those who love God, to those who are called according to His purpose."* Romans 8:28 NAS.

People opened their homes to us and I learned God's lesson of meekness. Once, while at the Laundromat, I glanced over to see a beat up looking man swagger over and sit next to my daughter, Tia—the Laundromat Evangelist! She started talking to him, her chubby little legs swung back and forth, never quite touching the floor while she sang a little tune. The man approached me and dug his hand into his dirty jean pocket. He pulled out a wrinkled dollar and a few coins. "Is that your little girl?" he asked. "Yes," I replied.

"I was about to use this money to buy another bottle of whiskey, but I was wondering if you would buy her a gift instead." A tear streamed down his dirty cheek. "She reminded me about Jesus and I need to make things right with Him."

Although we were without a home, God illustrated his love in many ways and provided for our needs. We didn't fall through the societal cracks, nor were we reported to Child Services.

* * *

My baby was missing and what scared me was I knew who had him. I was fortunate to know the police officer in charge. I put my trust in him and gave him the real scoop. Three days later my husband handed my baby to me. The officer told me to get my stuff together, put the kids in the car and never return. No money, no direction—I prayed. I drove to a new town and the people of one of the local churches loved on us and gave us hope!

My husband tracked us down. We moved again and we tried to make it work. Once again he established mob ties and during a drug deal gone badly, a "hit" was placed on our family. If he didn't return the money he had "borrowed," the kids and I would be killed. In order to save us he came home in the middle of the night and set our home on fire—hoping to collect the insurance money. But God had other plans. The fire did not ignite and we were sequestered away behind locked gates for our protection.

Meanwhile, my husband was on the run and out of time. The Lord had his attention and he was willing to yield. He prayed, "Lord, you know my life, if I continue to use, take me home and spare my family from this insanity." Standing before us he was washed and at peace. Being a new Christian he did what only he knew to do. He took a bottle of Wesson Oil and poured the entire bottle over my head. As oil dripped through my hair, over my face and down my neck I could feel his warm hands placed on my crown. His words were like honey and God's anointing enveloped me like rain. I could sense the Lord smiling on us as his heart burst forth blessing and protection over me. Turning to our children one by one, weeping my husband pleaded for understanding and forgiveness.

He was eager to join the Teen Challenge Drug Rehab program. For two weeks we prayed for a bed to become available for him. While we waited, the itch returned. Heroin wooed him and new friends lured him to join in for the one last hurrah. Death struck him that night. Yet, what Satan intended for evil God meant for good. At his funeral several people gave their hearts to the Lord.

It's been fourteen years since my husband's passing and God is still in control of my life with His healing, protection, blessings and grace. As a little girl, I longed to be loved and rescued and I grew up to find the One who valiantly participated in every event of my life. His love endures forever! Today I serve Him on the staff at my church and I continue to be available for whatever needs to be done behind the scenes at G.R.A.C.E. Ministries.

* * *

Not Just You

Tia's Song

Wake up in the morning I think like any other morning till I stepped out to see the sight. Turn and see a policeman and he's holding my mamma oh holding her so tight. Then the tears start flowing and I start knowing what evil went down that night. It must be my daddy for he hasn't come home; no he hasn't for quite some time.

Oh live your life and remember that it's just not you. There as so many watching and depending on a man like you.

The preacher started praying and voices started raisin as I just sat in my pew. They said he was a good man just not much of a plan when it comes to his life and starting new. People passed by as they started to cry shedding a tear for me too. Some shook their head and others said, "What is that little girl to do?"

Oh live your life and remember that it's just not you. There as so many watching and depending on a man like you.

Now I'm full grown and tried to get past what was sown in me those many years ago. Look back and sigh as a tear leaves my eye wishing you would have come home. Think of everything you missed, my wedding kiss and the child that you will never know. They may have your eyes but you'll never see inside 'cause you weren't there to see them grow.

Oh live your life and remember that it's just not you. There as so many watching and depending on a man like you.

Part III

What Makes Me a Christian?

Is it what I do?
> Is it what I see?

Is it who my friends are?
> Or is it just me?

Is it what I hear?
> Is it what I say?

Is it what I think?
> Or is it what I pray?

Is it because I go to church?
> Or that I love God?

Is it because of who I am?
> Or because he shed his blood?

Actually, the answer is
> All of the above

But what really helped me out,
Was God's eternal love.

John Bowles

How to Become a Christian

God loves us unconditionally and desires a personal relationship with us.

"For God so loved the world that he gave his only begotten Son, that whoever believes in him should not perish but have everlasting life." John 3:16 KJV.

Sin separates us from God. Confess and ask God to forgive your sins.

"For all have sinned and fall short of the glory of God." Romans 3:23 KJV.

Jesus paid the price for us on the cross when he died for our sins.

"But God demonstrates his own love for us in this: While we were still sinners, Christ died for us." Romans 5:8 NIV.

Jesus Christ did it all for us. All we have to do is accept his free gift.

"But to all who received him, who believed in his name, he gave power to become children of God." John 1:12 RSV.

A sample prayer to receive the free gift of salvation and become part of the family of God:

Father, I know I am a sinner. I believe you died for my sins, rose from the grave and are preparing a home in Heaven for me to spend eternity with you. I'm sorry for my sins. Please forgive me. Come into my life and take control of it. I trust you completely and accept your free gift of eternal life. Amen.

Welcome to the family of God!

You can be assured of your salvation:

"Behold, I stand at the door and knock; if any one hears my voice and opens the door, I will come in to him and eat with him, and he with me." Revelation 3:20 RSV.

That's the kind of relationship God desires to have with you.

By following these steps you will grow in your new faith:

- Tell someone about your new faith in Christ.
- Spend time with God each day – pray and read the Bible
- Seek fellowship with other Christians.

- Find a local church where you can worship God.
- Get baptized.

How to Write Your Story

Everyone has a story. As Christians, part of our story is our spiritual growth (called our testimony). It's as easy as 1-2-3 to write your story.

1. What your life was like before Christ came into it.
2. How you found Jesus Christ as your Savior.
3. What your life is like after you accepted Jesus' free gift of salvation.

Read Saul's (Paul's) story in Acts 9:1-19.

Before Paul's Conversion:

"But Saul, still breathing threats and murder against the disciples of the Lord, went to the high priest and asked him for letters to the synagogues at Damascus, so that if he found any belonging to the Way, men or women, he might bring them bound to Jerusalem." Acts 9:1-2 RSV.

Paul's Conversion:

"Now as he journeyed he approached Damascus, and suddenly a light from heaven flashed about him. And he fell to the ground and heard a voice saying to him, 'Saul, Saul, why do you persecute me?' And he said, 'Who are you, Lord?' And he said, 'I am Jesus, whom you are persecuting; but rise and enter the city, and you will be told what you are to do.' The men who were traveling with him stood speechless, hearing the voice but seeing no one. Saul arose from the ground; and when his eyes were opened, he could see nothing; so they led him by hand and brought him to Damascus. And for three days he was without sight, and neither ate nor drank." Acts 9:3-9 RSV.

After Paul's Conversion:

". . . For several days he was with the disciples at Damascus. And in the synagogues immediately he proclaimed Jesus, saying, 'He is the Son of God.' And all who heard him were amazed, and said, 'Is not this the man who made havoc in Jerusalem of those who called on this name? And he has come here for this purpose, to bring them bound before the chief priests.' But Saul increased all the more in

strength, and confounded the Jews who lived in Damascus by proving that Jesus was the Christ." Acts 9:19b-22 RSV.

Filled with the Holy Spirit as God's chosen instrument, Paul became a servant of Jesus Christ and shared his story with others, including Gentiles, kings and sons of Israel.

You may want to write several drafts of your story— adding experiences— how God changed your life, miracles you've witnessed, and answers to prayers. Your story may touch someone who has experienced similar experiences—a lost loved one, abuse, divorce, cancer, infertility, etc. How God brought you through major trials can be used by God to minister to others, offering them hope, encouragement, or insight. Add a Scripture verse that has ministered to you.

If you still feel you can't write your story, tell it to someone else and have them write it for you.

Afterward

"For the Son of man came to seek and to save the lost."
Luke 19:10 RSV.

God gave the G.R.A.C.E. Ministries leaders compassion for the lost and hurting women in Douglas County. Steve Green's song, "People Need the Lord," expresses their hearts towards the women in their community.

> Everyday they pass me by,
> I can see it in their eyes.
> Empty people filled with care, headed who knows where?

> On they go through private pain, living fear to fear.
> Laughter hides their silent cries,
> Only Jesus hears.

People need the Lord, people need the Lord.
At the end of broken dreams, He's the open door
People need the Lord, people need the Lord.
When will we realize, people need the Lord?

We are called to take His light
To a world where wrong seems right.
What could be too great a cost?
For sharing Life with one who's lost?

Through His love our hearts can feel
All the grief they bear.
They must hear the Words of Life
Only we can share.

People need the Lord, people need the Lord
At the end of broken dreams, He's the open door.
People need the Lord, people need the Lord.
When will we realize that we must give our lives?
For People need the Lord.

* * *

The women on the G.R.A.C.E. Ministries team knew their limitations, yet they were women of faith and knew personally the One who could do what they could not. *"Jesus looked at them and said, 'With man this is impossible, but with God all things are possible.'" Matthew 19:26 RSV.*

They followed God where He was leading them. *"For we are His workmanship, created in Christ Jesus for good works, which God prepared beforehand so that we would walk in them." Ephesians 4:6 NAS.*

"'For My hand made all these things, Thus all these things came into being,' declares the Lord. But to this one I will look, To him who is humble and contrite of spirit, and who trembles at My word.'" Isaiah 66:2 NAS.

By the grace of God and the power of the Holy Spirit, these humble women served where they believed God was leading them.

"Trust in the Lord with all your heart and lean not on your own understanding; in all your ways acknowledge him, and he will make your paths straight." Proverbs 3:5-6 NIV.

G.R.A.C.E. Ministries was founded on prayer. Ruth Fowler prayed even before she shared her vision of a Christian women's conference in Roseburg. Later the board joined her in praying and continued to pray throughout every aspect of planning and organizing the conference.

Women were encouraged to invite their neighbors, friends, co-workers and the women in their families. Sometimes others will listen to a speaker whereas they wouldn't step foot in a church for one reason or another.

They prayed during the conference for those working behind the scene as well as those visible—praying for those serving in worship, the speaker, and food preparation and service—that all would go smoothly and glorify God.

They also prayed after the conference for those who served—for their rest, refreshment and renewal. Their prayer included the women who attended as well as written prayer requests, and for the women whose lives were changed as a result of the conference—giving God the glory with hearts full of gratitude and thanks.

> Give thanks
> With a grateful heart
> Give thanks to the Holy One
> Give Thanks
> For He's given
> Jesus Christ, His Son

A Touch of Grace

And now let the weak say

I am strong

Let the poor say

I am rich

Because of what

The Lord has done

For us

Give thanks

Henry Smith

B.J.B

Breinigsville, PA USA
24 February 2011
256314BV00001B/3/P